Camus'
Camel

POETRY BY
JIM KELLER

Pinecone Book Company
P.O. Box 65 | Evergreen, Colorado 80437
PineconeBookCo@gmail.com

Dedicated to my wife,
Patricia Ann (Turnbull) Keller

Foreword

Concerning the title poem of this book, "Camus' Camel": A number of the words in the poem are derived from the titles of some of Albert Camus' works, including: "The Rebel," "The Stranger," "The Fall," "The Plague," "The Misunderstanding," and, of course, the made up verb, *sisypushed*, comes from Camus' "Myth of Sisyphus." Camus is often described as an existentialist and as the philosopher of the absurd, a word which describes the title poem and a number of the other poems herein.

In 1957, Albert Camus received the Nobel Prize in Literature. He died at the age of 46, three years later, in an auto accident. A camel was not involved.

Table of Contents

Camus' Camel

As a rebel
but not as a stranger
in Algeria
Camus acquired a Camel
with the standard accessories
a loathsome stench
and a plague of fleas
Nauseated by the smell
tormented by the fleas
blinded by the sun's glare
he rode
a beast!
into the desert
Until,
Camel halted
absurdly
below a dune
Whereupon, Camus dismounted
and sisypushed Camel
up the dune

while Camel brayed
that it was all a misunderstanding
this journey,
like life,
was meaningless
But at the top,
they toppled and
with the fall
Camel fell
on Camus
as they both rolled
to the bottom
and there died deaths
that also were meaningless
as one of them
which
I forget
had foretold.

Aegean Cruise

Kalimera!
My name is Odysseus
But you can call me Ody
because I know how hard Greek is
It took me years to learn it
and I was born in Ithaca
As you know today you are on your own
You can rest here on the ship or
you can come with me
to explore the ruins of Troy
a once great city
We Greeks have been falsely blamed
for its destruction,
through stratagem, it's said
But that's a baseless rumor
We were home in Greece at the time
arguing among ourselves

Zeus as Oncologist

So how do you feel today Prometheus?
Is the pain any better?
The MRI showed additional necrosis of your liver
I expected that the dosage of theodicy
I prescribed would have more efficacy.

But I see here on your chart that
you have been refusing to take it
In your condition it's silly to worry
about the side effects
And the cost is covered by your HMO
Besides, it is the strongest drug we have for
Aetos Kaukasios*
your type of cancer
You have only yourself to blame for
how badly things are going for you

* *The eagle Zeus set upon the bound Prometheus to daily eat his liver,
punishing the rebel titan for, among other things, giving fire to humans.*

Cerberus

You're dismissed Cerberus
There's nothing to guard here now
The mortgage is foreclosed
Hell's shut and padlocked
Failure of Croesus' bank
has led to this the
ultimate bankruptcy
It was ever thus with plutocracies
A hundred million cemeteries are the creditors
But there's nothing of value to claim

And you shades must go
Move lively now you homeless wisps
you heroes and cowards, kings and thieves
mass murderers and saints
All even now
The boundless ether's your new home
Aeolus will drive you
everywhere and evermore

Now guard yourself Cerberus
Keep watch and listen
with the eyes and ears of all your heads
for the Great Dog Catcher in the sky
Your license expired 20 centuries ago

Before He Got Into Astronomy, Ptolemy Had a Real Job, as a Welder

It was colder then, when,
what people incorrectly call the Sun,
the daily renewing of the sky's joint
hammer welded by the Great Artificer,
who, overcoming initial clumsiness,
got quite good
and made the daily seaming of the sky
reasonably straight and true,
though you could still see the joint
if you squinted and turned your head sideways

That was the Bronze Age
The sky was translucent but golden-hued
The Artificer's fresh joint glowed dimly
and men were heroes
(Or at least heroic braggarts;
some even claimed to be gods)

As technology improved
the job could be subcontracted
and Artificer received a promotion to a distant galaxy
to do less tedious things for a less savage people

She still had quality assurance responsibility for Earth, though
and arranged to receive regular, dated and certified reports
from counterchecking Egyptian and Mayan priests, who
between supervising the laborious construction
of pointy piles of stone
wasted much time gazing at the sky

So before leaving
Artificer solicited proposals

from all the gods' men
and all the men's gods

But it was a scruffy journeyman welder,
name of Helios
who won the job,
Of course, he had low-balled the bid,
figuring to make it up on change orders, and
knowing full well he'd have to pay below minimum wage
and use undocumented and child labor
Helios' bid specified that
the weld would be made by torch;
oxy-acetylene was the favored technology
albeit Olympian OSHA bureaucrats
stubbornly insisted on MAPP
causing the first costly change order

Though his sire tried hard to train him
and beat him regularly,
Phaeton was a desultory student
who never passed his license test
or even got an apprentice card
The thoroughbreds who pulled the welding cart despised
the sulky adolescent
who mucked never a stall clean

So when Helios went on a binge
with his drinking buddy Dionysus,
(who couldn't seem to run out of wine,
or crazed groupies for that matter)
Phaeton had no possibility to control the big,
high-compression H-4
Oh, the weld was ugly that day
It went up and forth and back and down

There was weld slag and liquid metal everywhere
dripping down, falling to earth
but mostly on revelers in Lebanon,
where Mardi Gras played all year long,
and the next-door jealous prudes of Israel,
the bible belt in those days,
said the lot of them deserved it
The sky was stitched so poorly
that much of the atmosphere leaked away
leaving so little oxygen
that heroism
(but not heroic bragging)
is nearly impossible since
That's when Artificer warp sped back
reined in the horses, reversed the cart
and drove backwards to back-weld the seam
which caused apoplexy and even suicides
among the silly and the superstitious

Next She engaged an Athenian firm
Socrates, Plato, Aristotle and Peripatetic Associates
to abrogate the contract with Helios and sue for damages
Of course, Helios skipped and hasn't been heard from since
though some say he's in the cattle business
in Rhodes or maybe Sicily

A guy with the peculiar name of Phoebus Apollo
had been the second lowest bidder
so the contract was next awarded to him
Though inexperienced
he was a brainy sort
with a Ph. D. and post-doc work
in psycho-neuro-self analysis
(Relativity is more widely understood)

At first Apollo continued using the horses and cart, but
after the run up in oat futures during the Peloponnesian war,
he sold the equines and cart to the Valkyries,
a bitchy, butchy equestrian club from up North,
and he converted the torch to natural gas
from an Olympian Limited Partnership well
he controlled near Delphi
taking the legal depletion allowance and thereby
earning a nice, mostly tax-free return on both investments

Later he outsourced an R & D contract to a handy guy,
name of Hephaestus,
The latter had been a defense contractor, but,
what with the hero shortage,
had turned to beating out plows, roto-tillers
and other farm implements from scrapped swords
armor, spearheads and other surplus Trojan War junk

Together Ap & Heph worked out the present contrivance
with the automatic orbital welder rotating around the Earth
at precisely 3.03 microradians per second
and using 10 trillion megawatts of heat lightning for
the Tungsten/Argon Inert Gas (TIG) arc

Apollo's Delphic operating instructions
tended toward the dangerously ambiguous
so Hephaestus codified the procedures
into the ASME pressure vessel welding specifications
(Book VIII, Chapter IV, Section 3)

Quality control was left to the aforementioned priests for a while
But like all clerics, they got diverted into theological disputes
which of course, escalated into armed conflicts
(splitting doctrinal hairs with war axes)
thereby neglecting their more important duty
prompting Ap to purchase a robotic
Cosmic X-Ray Inc. Visualizer machine
which normally follows right behind the welder
though occasionally it gets a little ahead and causes eclipses
(which gets the sillies all worked up again)
This system works quite well, the Great Artificer is satisfied,
though She responsibly cares about the atmosphere's argon
    buildup,
which the latest gas chromatography/mass spectroscopy
    analyses show
is now nearly up to a gnarly 1%
(The EPA is looking into a regulation requiring a reduction
of the arc welder's emissions of inert gas.)

Apollo's now in retirement on Delos, where he grew up
With his sister, Artemis, he competes in coed archery contests
on the seniors' circuit,
and he swims with dolphins in a show for tourists
He dines out a lot at nectar and ambrosia bars, which,
because of the free-range supernatural food craze, are
very pricey now
So Apollo's tab overwhelms the monthly
distributions from his Roth IRA
and since immortality lasts a long time
Midas, his financial adviser, is naturally concerned.

Looking Down on an Icy Sea
from 30,000 Feet

Not opaque and white with snow
like the pack ice near shore
pieces of nascent sea ice
are transparent as glass
as if Odin had passed this way and
clumsy for a god,
dropped the brand new window pane
for his ice palace
and saw it shatter into shards
on the slate-gray sea.

Zeus as a Rape Counselor

Danae, a beautiful princess, was the daughter of Acrisius,
King of Argos, whom the Delphic Oracle prophesied would
die at the hand of his grandson. Thus, Acrisius confined
Danae in a bronze tower to retain her virginity. However,
Zeus, smitten with Danae, transforming himself into a shower
of gold, visited her and impregnated her. She bore a son,
Perseus. Furious, Acrisius cast mother and son out to sea
in a wooden chest, which floated ashore on the Isle of Seriphos,
where they were rescued. Years later, the adult Perseus threw
a discus which accidentally killed his grandfather.

Danae get hold of yourself
I'm sorry you're distressed
but try to calm down
Being emotional about this doesn't help
We need to get through this interview

Let me review with you
my notes of what you've told me.
You were locked in a tower
taking a shower
a golden shower—you said
What do you mean by
a golden shower?
Was the water yellow?
Are you sure it was just water?
Oh, you weren't taking a shower.
You were fully clothed
when the alleged attack occurred.

But were you dressed provocatively?
Oh, the alleged perpetrator removed your clothes
Did you help him?

Now don't get upset.
I need to follow this checklist for the record

So he must have broken or unlocked the door.
Or did you do that?

I'm sorry.
I have to ask these questions.

But your tunic was easily removed.
wouldn't you agree?
Is that when he showered you with gold?

Did you take the gold?
If you did, we'd have to call it something
other than rape wouldn't we?

Oh the shower of gold entered you?
(That's to a strange purse)
Oh, it wasn't real gold
and it made you pregnant?
Yes I would say it was definitely other than gold.

And then your father grew angry with you.
(Fathers usually get upset with unwed pregnant daughters.)
and set you and your son adrift on the sea
in a wooden chest, whereby
you landed here at Seriphos, unharmed!

Danae this tale of yours
is so strange and confusing
I don't know how to help you.
You claim to have been raped
in a locked tower

You can't describe the perpetrator
and you claim to have received gold
that wasn't really gold
and it made you pregnant.

I can't imagine taking this case to the Council.
They would laugh at you
throw you out
Danae I think you just have to accept
you have no legal recourse in this matter
But you're young and attractive
You should be able to find a husband
and a father for your son
He's a bright boy
and strikingly handsome
I find myself strangely drawn to Perseus
I expect great things of him

I Talked with God the Other Day

He wasn't busy
I guess Pat Robertson and George Bush
were bothering someone else
I asked Him how two meters
of DNA can fit into
each human cell whose diameter
is a millionth of that.
He said He couldn't figure it out either
It must be Evolution

Neutrinos

Recognizing
the imperfections in this
her first
and our cosmos
the shamed Demiurge
moved on
creating other, improved universes
in the strings of 666 dimensions
and ignored us
with the evil
and those damned neutrinos

An April Fool and a Weeping God

'Twas on an April's eve
deep in a dream that night
that mutated suddenly,
from images benign
and well known to me
to a horror, a visage indescribable
I shuddered, but didn't wake
It was a god I felt,
somehow, I knew
a god that wept, a knowing god
But why?
And forming the question in my mind
was only required, for Its answer came
resounding back as a primal roar,
reverberating within the great rotunda of my skull

"I weep for you, for yours and for me
For just as you of all the animals
ken mortality,
I know even that much more.
I see doom and doomsday for us all
But you in your happy naiveté
can yet smile and laugh a time
Meanwhile
we gods do appear only in dreams
and speak only in obscurities
For other than that
you could not endure"

I thanked It then
and in my distress
made a small trite jest
The answer was an anguished howl
as It departed me
and I realized then
that It could never laugh
Its omniscience
precluded any jocularity
just as my innocence
prevented interminable weeping

So those of us who would be gods
are asking what we oughtn't
and gods would gladly exchange with us
and bear the gentler burden of our ignorance

Grim Visage

Greetings grim visage,
who is always there
when I close my eyes.
You alone give form
to that dark landscape.
Inverse silhouette,
dimly luminous,
barely perceived
Two eyes faintly
watching
A mouth always
silent
Are you my soul?
Are you Yahweh,
or Lucifer.
Or an angel
by one of them
assigned to me?

How do you judge me?
Have I done
what I could?
Will I be
what I should?
Do you know
my destiny?
When I die
will you
move on
to watch another?
Will I in turn
become
a ghastly
ghostly face
extant only
in a mind's eye?

The Shrike

My gods were birds
Oh they could soar on wings of grace
But in ones and twos
I called them down to earth
They came all trusting
What had they to fear, being gods
They sat down beside me
And when they began to sing
I listened all enthralled, for a time
Their separate songs began in loving harmonies
but diverged as they expostulated theologies
So very soon there was cacophony,
and a most annoying dissonance
Since I had gained their confidence
and they were unvigilant in their busy dissension
I snatched them, one by one
and impaled them on
the thorns of my locust tree
Oh, they were surprised
They struggled for a while
and then died without understanding
Now when their desiccated bodies
flutter in the wind
their wings snap open
They seem about to take flight
But the thorns hold them
I was careful
Sometimes I pick at the carcasses
but there's no sustenance there
just beaks and horny vellum
and moldering bones

Blackie

Many who have spent a lifetime
can tell us less of love than
the child that lost a dog yesterday.
—Thornton Wilder

Black spot ahead

Black fur

A Labrador's down
in the weeds of the shoulder

We slow and see
no movement there

A child will cry tonight

Blackie isn't coming home

Business Trip to Gillette

Easter Tuesday,
I ascended
unwillingly resurrected
from the winter dead plains
A lonely planet waiting
raced the plane North
over a long dark cloud
We lost
but won
Gillette!
Bleak!
The damn wind!
Why come here?
Is ennui so rare?
Weary!
A Pleistocene glacier
ground me down
My transmission failed
so many frequent flyer miles ago
long before thought
of product warranties
But mortgages concentrate
the mind

And my clients
brilliant
pay me
enough
said
But what's this job to do with
"The Ascent of Man"
by Bronowski, on PBS
Sunday nights at 8 o'clock

Annuities are safe and sure
gambles for your dotage
which ends puberty
at last
Unelected,
nonetheless
Chance governs,
We the governed dance
staggering exhausted
to a dirge
Ashes, ashes
we all fall down

El Chucho

A car door closes softly, but
El Chucho hears and barks
Carlos roused from sleep, gets up
opens the door to the ICE men
several and large
El Chucho barks again and growls
to complain of their entering his house
But Carlos shakes his finger at him
and points to his bed
He goes tail down, reluctantly
continuing to growl
and watch the men
now in his house
speaking a strange,
harsh tongue

Awake, the family
begins gathering their things
into black garbage bags
Maria helping the children

At last a man opens the door
Carlito and Angelina
bawling, hug their Chucho
before leaving the house
Outside El Chucho tries to follow
But Carlos sternly says No!
and points to the backyard
El Chucho goes only to the side of the house
watches his family taken away
in the dark vans

Now El Chucho sleeps under his car
against a wheel that blocks
the wind and the snow
Food left by Little Carlos and Angelina
is gone
as is the water
He is cold, hungry and very thirsty
El Chucho cries
But no one hears who cares

Till Death Do Us Part - I

Younger then, I waited
flushed and naked in my bed
for the cadence on the stair's ascent
of my heavy booted lover

And now ....
it's late, and dark
but he will come home,
drunk and raging at a world
whose emissary I am
and strangely, by
his appointment
And I in my complicity
will be held accountable
for all the slights and slurs
the denials and defeats
Somehow they are of my doing
An abler wife could heal
these hurts of her man
But not such as I

So now as I hear the lurching thud
of his brute boots upon the stairs
I lie breathless, trembling
and pray that, this time, he'll just
rape me

Till Death Do Us Part - II

It was ages ago
we were in our prime
she was ravishing, and so
I ravished her

Later, our love was
no less erotic, no less violent
to which it seemed, she assented
There were problems, sure
a demeaning job brought home for her to share
the solutions I sought in alcohol and drugs
but we made it all up in bed
And bruises are gone in a week or two,
the cracked rib in a month
There was the orbital fracture,
That did heal slowly
But her complaints were muted,
hardly memorable
The Church only, she claims now,
prevented her escaping me
It seemed more secular, sexual at the time

But now in this, my last and final stage
of old age and a wasting disease
I ken how much she resented,
nay, even hated me!
And for that I pay dearly
For she is now much the stronger
These useless purple-white sticks
which had the strength of three,
cannot even raise me
and these emaciated legs
will never again be socketed

in the work boots moldering under this bed
So now as I lay here bathed in my filth,
I shudder, for I know,
when she comes,
her rage,
like my incontinence,
will engulf me,
and she will pummel me,
returning with interest those blows,
that I'd only lent her,
so long ago,
when she was young
and I was a beast

So now as I hear the click of her heels
in the hall outside my room
I lie breathless, trembling
and pray that this time, this time
she will kill me.

Day of the Whirlwind,
Knight of the Rake

Assembling the leaves of a prior year
abruptly the faded shades resurrected,
began to dance in frenzy
and leaping higher still
gave form to mine old enemy
a surly tower of swirling brown

"Dust devil, Son of Chaos
leave my leaves alone
else I will joust with you
and run you through"

An insolent bluster was his response
Incensed at that, I set my lance,
the rake
Quixote-like I charged
and struck
impaled him there
But me he swallowed and enveloped
along with the frenzied leaves
He tried to turn me then
to twist me like the grasses
to shake me like the bushes
to dance me like the leaves
But I was too stark!
Knights of the Rake
are not as the grasses
or the bushes
or the leaves

Emboldened now, I held firmly
and began to parry and thrust

"I have you now windwhirl
you shan't steal my leaves
Be done oh windy one
For you I'll best anon"

A banshee wail was his response
and the tower that was he
lurched and leaned
spilling some of my leaves

Disheartened now
he tried to spin away from me
but with my worthy weapon
I pursued and raked him horribly

Sorely wounded he windspered

"Leave me be"

But I would nothing of it
And thrusting again my terrible lance
I disemboweled him there
He expired, with a windper

And with his death
so the leaves
obedient now
floated
down
landing
each
in turn
at
my
feet

Smartly I reversed my weapon
and returned to
assembling the leaves of a prior year

Chocolate

Eating an ice cream cone
at the Flamenco Yacht Basin
just a stop on our tour
I hold it up and glance beyond
The chocolate color matches that
perfect and permanent tan
of an elegant woman
Cool and sweet,
perfectly blended
of the best ingredients
that Panama can provide
She fits right in
to this place of wealth and privilege
She's seated on a bench with a man
her husband or her pimp
I'm guessing the latter
For in this locale
and in this Darwinian world
such a woman is too rare
and would be shared

Now she boldly returns my stare
and I avert my eyes
to concentrate on the chocolate
of my cone

Normandy

Lush grasses grace the berms of graves
o'erlooking the strand that slayed these men
If they could but see they would perceive
a roiling, untamed sea, not unlike
that which bore them in their blatant boats
to dire foes' fire and eternity

Not far off the whitecaps mark the shallows
where their boats struck and foundered
where German guns first drew aim and blood

But the real killing ground was the beach
It offered no shelter, no succor

The grass hairs the graves of the brave
of men by themselves given little chance
of dead men unremembered now
except by a failing few.

Finger Lakes Glove

Homeward bound
and looking down
from 30,000 feet and nostalgia
on five bloodless fingers
shivering in February cold
under skin of gray-white ice
and the palsied palm with graves I've known
west of my time-warped,
canal-spawned Syracuse,
as so often, strewn with snow
but black creased by its newer lifeline,
the longer-lived Thruway

And just then, slowly creeping
from the south, I see
a gray and gossamer glove
knitted and purled in the Catskills
by spectral thunder-headed grandmothers
from the wooly remnants of a Nor'easter
as they chattered in Yiddish
while watching their great, great grandbabies
skate on the pond at Grossingers

And I watched, while
the shivering hand pulled on the glove
up each finger lake, carefully
so as not to tear the tender ground fog,
which trapping the meager irradiance
of the fingers, forestalls further frostbite

By now over Rochester, I stare back
at the hand in the glove,
no doubt warmer, happier now,
no longer cursing the winter,
but like me, thinking ahead
to another spring
when frozen arthritic fingers
will thaw and become live and fluent again.

Cadillac Coupe de Ville

That stately black Cadillac Coupe de Ville moves
languidly crossing two lanes through the lengthy left turn
devouring its due time and mine of the green arrow
It's now too late for me
behind in my blue Suburu
to turn too
even though I warned him
of the arrow punctually
with my horn
tardy as I am getting to work

I know Cadillac man by his personalized license plate,
Wilson1, he's the one I've waited on
and there's the Coupe de Ville with all deliberate speed
still moving away with pomp and no circumstance
interminably down the long straight street
I see anon Wilson1's bald pink profile
plump with yet another indulgence
He's unhurried, he doesn't have to get to work
His money works for him, even as I work for mine
His money is always on the job
It never sleeps, though he sleeps soundly!
Compounding round the World
it follows the Sun in foreign hedge funds
and shows itself with interest to him each morn
always bigger and more exuberant
like a hyperactive adolescent Saint Bernard
Wilson1 doesn't have to commute
He chose to dawdle during rush hour
only because it is his right
It is clear he has nowhere to go
and no reason to get there
His money is already there

Tectonic Spite

That one's far away now
beyond the curve of the earth
Not even our mountains can sneer

But see those beings yonder
there in the harbor town
bent to their business
with savage persistence
eyes downcast, minds set
in cement of resentment
Yesterday, as stranger there,
was salutation yours?
Did one lift glass with you
or meet your eye
except with hostile stare?
In the dingy inn, did you elect
the chair backed 'gainst the wall?

Yes, there's a wrath in this land
It's that, you've sensed
And if you would know
this is whence
it was come
This long berm 'pon which you stand
haired with billowing grass
and crowning the curving cape
appears rather like a welt
raised on a giant's arm
And so I am, in a way
But a welt turned to purpose
to a weapon
Look there where I dip
to meet the uneasy sea

and appear to end, well
that's deceitful, of me
I persist submerged
for another league
There's my serrated blade
you see only my hand-worn hilt
A sword for sailors is what I am
and many there are that have felt my edge
upon rounding yonder cape

But my story starts eons ago
a thousand million years
when this continent was coupled to another
Their separation was angry, violent
And from a grievous wound
made here by the other
I flowed
red-hot basalt gore
I seared everything,
everything in my path
Ah, then was no deceit!
Until my temper cooled a whit
and I began to clot
in great vertical hexagonal prisms
to become a frozen scab
a wrathful witness of that wound
and of a craton's infidelity

And that rancor still persists
For when emissaries,
ships of men, come
from that perfidious one,
unused to these waters
and innocent of history like you,
oft are they caught on my blade
and the malicious creatures you see
like ravenous crabs to a beached sea bass
swarm to the smashed wreck
and pillage the bones of the ship
And if there've been survivors
of those many hapless mariners
they haven't trod this berm

Thus is vengeance taken
for that unforgiven abandonment
so long ago.

Labrador Gone

Almost anywhere
along this desolate road
we could have stopped to change drivers
Where we did
the happy lab saw new playmates,
picked up his ragged tennis ball
and wagged across his yard
and into the road
where the 18 wheeler
never saw him and
didn't feel the impact
The lab had no time to yelp
either as he and his ball flew,
the last time he would chase it

We knocked at the door
of the lonely house
and informed the woman who answered
We tried to comfort her
before driving away
as she stood in the road
over her dead friend
tears flowing down her face
her sorrow shaded with anger
at our stupid choice

So Much Depends On A Red Pickup

Double high and coming up behind,
playing checkers
swerving out around and jumping like a king
the drizzle-glistened mostly white or black sedans
They're back in the bone yard now
behind my blue Suburu and
the cowboy with a gunrack, raised suspension
and balloon tires
Impatiently it weaves across the line to spy ahead
then scuttles back, retracting the move
Is that within the rules?
But then a trifling pause in opposing traffic
it guns beside me
No cowboy
But bouffant blonde cowgirl
with assertive gaze, darts in ahead
jumping me and
bumper tagging the next jumpee
Her scarlet Ramcharger has a smashed taillight
Wonder how anyone caught her from behind?
But now I see the bumper sticker
A HARD MAN IS GOOD TO FIND

i as the square root of - 1

*A complex number has a real part and an imaginary part.
The imaginary part contains the square root of -1, designated
as i. Thus X = A + Bi is a complex number with A as a real
number and Bi as the imaginary part.*

We all live our days on the infinite plane
of complex numbers: minus x to plus x,
minus yi to plus iy.
Most of us
cling close as real numerals
along the x axis, acting positively or negatively.
Occasionally, i take short excursions
standard deviations
up or down into imaginary domains
where the square root of minus one dominates.
But my existence is mostly
linear, i don't feel comfortable
without some grounding in reality.
This quibble's
lost on my bipolar friend
He needs not the mooring of the real integers
Recently i watched him
on an emotional hyperbola in iy
He screamed along ever closer to a hard asymptote
on the way to iy infinity
A femtosecond later he was back
approaching the x axis
at relativistic velocity
Foreshortened he whipped around the focus
waving ever so slowly at me and enduring
without concern a colossal centrifugal force
Next he's out on the other arm of the conic section
testing the limits of minus yi.

At such times i try to calm him
with a damping function.
It sometimes works
He has lucid moments,
talks about the weather,
current events and
other real functions of x.

But a moment later,
he's off again
into imaginary space.
He scares me then,
i don't understand him
And safe on the x axis,
i watch transfixed, as a constant
While he, a Jacobian
of an exponential variable,
moves on his limitless plane of being
and soars on the wings of i.

Labrador Lost

I passed him at sixty-five
walking on the shoulder
panting and limping a bit
As lost as he is black
on this interstate
Maybe someone forgot him
at a rest stop
He's following behind
as fast as he can
If he strays into a traffic lane
he's a goner
He's like Limbo and Bruiser
and Kimbu and even
Preacher Cassels
All dead now
except for him
He was alive a mile ago
He's one of them
and all of them
Maybe he was looking for me

God as a Gunship

The Associated Press
Sarajevo, Bosnia-Herzegovina—Captain Albert J.
Brown, whose F-16 jet was downed last week by a
Serb missile, was rescued today from a Bosnian
forest by helicopter-borne U.S. marines. "God
answered my prayers," Brown said.

Meanwhile in other action in Bosnia, a mortar shell
lobbed into Sarajevo by Serb forces surrounding
the city, exploded, killing three-year-old Dragisa
Dizdarevic, playing nearby.

I heard God striding through angry clouds
his voice thundering in staccato,
the beat of His beneficence
His angels, NATO Christian soldiers
marching as to peacekeeping
in blessed robes of camouflage,
haloed by helmets
hallowed by purpose
bid me hurry to His waiting arms
the gunship, fiery chariot
of His omnipotence
Thus found, cradled, retrieved to His glory
I gave joyous thanks for
my earnest prayers answered
my erstwhile faith rewarded

The Lord hears the pious
the faithful, the peacekeepers
He safeguards His people, the righteous
Only evildoers, faithless apostates
need fear the stochastic mortar shells

57 Ford Fairlane

It stood next to the import that ran
two-toned, chalking creme
and crimson fading to pink
Two tires were flat and
the rear window was cracked
Remember fender skirts?
Well they always rusted first
These formed two auburn eyebrows
over the heavy-lidded wheels

She came out with him then
"Now remember, don't forget
when the washer stops
put the clothes in the dryer
I've made the settings
All you have to do is load it
and close the door
You ought to be able to do that
much!
And when are you gonna
get rid of that wreck?
It doesn't work
We don't need two cars,
now that you're retired and don't work."
He didn't answer
She got in the Nissan and left
on her errand
He watched them as they turned the corner
his hand resting on the Fairlane's fender
as if to caress it

Huntin' Trucks and Ducks

Hatched new in dark metallic shades
they're chalking now
to grudging Easter egg pastels
Road kill vultures lined up fender to battered fender
parked in the rutted mud
their grills in rusted crippled grins
each with two headlights unlit
but staring over the grey-green marsh
(except for one, made one eyed
in unforeseen collision)
watching for their hunting buddies
wet muddy dogs and smoking, cussing men
and their prey
mallards
who moments before secure
in the fellowship of their flock
with colors burnished by slanting sun
were wheeling round on the wind
till a God-like shout
flung them from the air
each an Icarus into the marsh
and now, bloody and broken
yellow bills gasped open in death
they're thrown in the backs
of the rusting trucks
with the dogs
and the garbage bound for the dump

It Was for the Children

It was for the children
that we married that bleak March
acquaintances imitating sweethearts
Missed punctuation made the sentence
or we never would have served it
He never said that he was scared

It was for the children
that we practiced role reversal
children acting like parents
Stage directions were vague
the playwright was drunk
He never said that he was unhappy

It was for the children
that we stayed together
strangers miming lovers
with passion declining
even with liquor assisting
He never said that he was desperate

It was for the children
that we battled each other
parents aping gladiators
the children were frightened
but we made them choose sides
He never said that he would beat me

It was for the children
that we separated
a family pretending no longer
But he couldn't stand it
and found us at the shelter
He never said that he would kill me

It was for the children

My Stomach, My Friend
(A guttural study)

Disgruntled, when I
its amicable advice ignored,
my stomach growled and grumbled, while I
gobbled chips and salsa
gulped Chimichanga
chugged dos Dos Equis

Kept up all night, even as
I slept soundly and tight
it ranted and rumbled
trying gastrin and pepsin
bile and trypsin to solve
the postdoc biochemistry
of that problematical repast

In the morning bleakness
of my awakeness
I could feel its rancor
and taste its sour disposition
To placate it,
I fed it
granola and yogurt
Which grudgingly it accepted
Such gestures
are obligatory, for I
must get going, and,
like an army of Gauls,
travel on my stomach

Nora

*In 1931, James Joyce married Nora
Barnacle at the Kensington Registry
Office in London. They had been living
together for 26 years.*

So Nora
wielding her wiles
clung like a barnacle
to the genius
showing no jealousy
of Molly Bloom,
Joyce's long-winded
daydreaming heroine, knowing
though comely
Molly was completely
lacking in compunction
or punctuation
going on and on
both impregnable
yes
and without a period
yes

Hygiene

(In the end
microbes
vital to our digestion
will digest
us in turn)

We evolved living amongst
the disgusting detritus
of filthy caves
our proto-toddlers crawling
among the rotting remnants
of recent repasts
competing with the incumbent rodents
to teethe on the bones of extinct ungulates

Our viscera contain in numbers
vaster than our bodies' cells
the descendants of the prokaryotic
bacteria and archaea
that co-evolved with us in those caves

Our coexistence with these microbes
is necessary if not always benign
(Lovers must quarrel occasionally
in order to renew their vows)
And without such occasional stimuli
it is said our immune systems
would be profoundly asleep when we're
attacked by less felicitous bugs

All this is well known to you so
why do you importune me so vehemently
to clean up this small mess I've made?

Silk Road

Come now to
the Han Dynasty
where wriggling worms
feasting on mulberry leaves
produce gossamer filaments
spun and woven by Han women
into the sheerest of fabrics
folded into packs of
two–humped Bactrians
assembled in caravans and driven
plodding over scalding sands
of the Gobi
and then north of the Pamir
to beckoning Uzbekistan
Tashkent and Samarkand
thence to Persia and finally
to Italy
for Roman women of
classic Italic voluptuousness
draped in the clinging silk
viewed hungrily by virile gladiators
in the Coliseum before
they clash and die

Little Collateral Damage

We know that President Saddam is a psychopath
that he has weapons of mass destruction
and he will use them on us if we let him
But President Bush has directed that
our weapons are to destroy his weapons
before that murderer can react

And this war is not being fought like other wars
This war is about technology
and we have it and the enemy doesn't
We have smart bombs and missiles
with GPS guidance systems
We are delivering special gifts to that maniac
Gifts that find targets within a twenty-foot circle
Now that's accuracy
Mark me here!
We will do everything,
to ensure that
there will be little collateral damage

Fatima had wanted to leave Baghdad
but being great with child
made it difficult to travel
She did not want to have the baby
in a village with poor sanitation
and without a doctor
So she stayed with her Mother
close to the hospital
The Americans don't bomb hospitals

But no one puts a hospital in a wasteland,
in a desert
A hospital must be in a city
near the people
near targets
And the smart bomb smartly hit the target
a Republican Guard barracks
near the hospital
The blast leveled the barracks
and blew in the windows
on that side of the hospital
where Fatima had just had her baby
and was holding her
as the shards of glass killed her
she who was as yet unnamed
But we can call her
Little Collateral Damage

Assumption

My assumption has always been that
the Catholic high school for boys
in East Saint Louis had a modest success
in educating
some pretty fine young men
although they seemed
to get a bit rowdy
when released on Fridays
from under the thumbs of the nuns and
out of reach of their knuckle-busting rulers

But good things always end and
Assumption High School
was retired forever in 1989
making it difficult for alumni
to revisit their school and
relive their formative years there
although
a select few got that opportunity
when the State purchased the facility
from the diocese turning it into
The Southern Illinois Correctional Center
adding a sturdier fence,
but only slightly modifying
its correctional methods

One More Flea on Darwin's Monkey

We all agreed
it was the right thing to do

Her appearance was aberrant
Her hair covered by a scarf
Her clothes were odd
Her shoes weren't black
She wore amulets and fetish symbols
She called them jewelry
We all agreed
they were hex signs

Her behavior was abhorrent
She didn't attend our meetings
She claimed to know the true faith
Another faith
It told her what to do
and she did it
mumbling nonsense
prostrating herself
intoning strange chants
We all agreed
they were wicked

Her companions were like her
They were strange
None of us knew them or wanted to
They kept to themselves
rejecting our overtures
They worshiped as she did
We all agreed
they were apostates

She sometimes talked to children
That was dangerous
She could tell them incorrect things
or teach them dangerous science
We all agreed
we couldn't have that

After vespers on that night
we found her and her group
gathered together in contravention
of our laws and customs
We arrested them
and held them in jail
We let most of them go
We're not a vindictive people
We can show God's mercy
But we had
to make an example of their leader
We had
to make the others
understand the error
of their practices
their beliefs
We all agreed
they needed a lesson

She was whipped
and given five years
She had a child
but someone took care of it
one of her group, I think
They moved away
all of them
We haven't missed them
They never fit in.
We're glad we got rid of them

We all agreed
it was the right thing to do

Symposia
(From Greek, drinking parties)

In a fragment from his c. 375 BC play *Semele* or *Dionysus*, Eubulus has
the god of wine Dionysus describe proper and improper drinking:
*For sensible men I prepare only three kraters: one for health (which they
drink first), the second for love and pleasure, and the third for sleep. After
the third one is drained, wise men go home. The fourth krater is not mine
any more—it belongs to bad behavior; the fifth is for shouting; the sixth is
for rudeness and insults; the seventh is for fights; the eighth is for breaking
the furniture; the ninth is for depression; the tenth is for madness and
unconsciousness.* From Wikipedia

A diligent student
I attended many symposia as an undergrad at Illinois
Some were at Bidwell's
which smelled even before you entered
of beer and smoke
occasionally vomit
The names of other drinking establishments
have escaped me after a half century
But they were no worse
or better

Ignorant of the real Greeks
we knew nothing of Dionysus
and his kraters of wine
Pitchers of beer were familiar
on which unluckily
the god'd placed no limits
though his krater numbers
may have pertained

Entertainment at our symposia
consisted of drinking songs
sung a cappella
and dissonant after the third pitcher

I still remember many of the libretti
though I dare not sing them
in this refined age

I remember one symposium at Bidwell's
when I exceeded Dionysus'
recommendations and
trying to impress a girl
showed how hard it was
to crush a hard-boiled egg in one's hand

Unluckily the egg I chose was an interloper
unboiled
placed among the boiled
by a malevolent prankster
When crushed
it sprayed its liquid contents on us

That was our last date

I'm told there were more serious symposia
discussing difficult topics
at other venues on campus where
hypotheses were proposed,
discussed, attacked, defended,
accepted or discarded.

But I didn't attend any of those symposia.

The Demise of Jacques La Glace

New York Times News Service
*Jacques La Glace, acclaimed impresario of the silver
screen, died yesterday in his Midtown apartment—
broke and alone—a victim of violence. Police stated
they have no suspects. Mssr. La Glace never went out;
he saw only those people who came to see him, and
there is no trace of them or their visits. The following
statement was found among his remains:*

I have mimed reality
as truly as ever was done
My viewers trusted in that
They had learned to appreciate
my representation of their daily lives
My critics have me maligned
saying I peopled my world
with too many left-handers
A grievous fault
I concede
upon reflection
But God has skewed the laws of symmetry
and even my talent
could not amend them
Dyslexics loved me better
They saw no discrepancy in my view
I loved them back, for we are kin

But only Charlie Dodgson
the great logician
could truly fathom my world
He alone mirrored my thinking
and got within my work

So my world's in shards
And now I'm gone.
I brought vantage afore
I'll bring woe anon

Heirlooms

This watch reads a half hour slow
It's too damn complicated to change it
Easier to change the time in my head
It was my father's watch
The wrist band is much too long
I got my small bones from my mother
my brain from my father I hope
She got Alzheimer's
along with her three sisters
This is a Seiko watch
self-winding
wound by my movement
It'll keep going for a few hours
after my heart stops ticking
My heart is from my father I think

End Notes

Acknowledgements

Thanks to the editors of the magazines where some of these poems first appeared, some in slightly different form: *Poetry City*, *Porter Gulch Review*, *Verse Virtual*, *Mad Blood*.

Special Thanks

To a small group of very exceptional poets who tolerated and worked futilely to remedy my lack of talent and understanding: **Joe Hutchison**, **Rita Brady Kiefer**, **Murray Moulding**, **Sandra McRae Sajbel** and **Padma Thornlyre**.

Cover Design

By my wife, **Patricia Ann (Turnbull) Keller**, a true artist.

Author's Bio

Jimmy (Jim) Keller retired in 2014 after working 53 years as a chemical engineer. One of his retirement projects was to write more poetry and gather together what he'd written over the previous quarter century. This book is a product of that project.

Concerning Jacques La Glace

The late Jacques La Glace, of course, was a mirror. And Charlie Dodgson is better known as Lewis Carroll, author of *Through the Looking Glass*.

Made in the USA
San Bernardino, CA
08 June 2020